A PACKI
CRACK_Rs

Edmund Banyard

**Seven Sketches looking at Gospel truths
from a fresh angle**

No performance of this play may be given without the written permission of the publisher to whom all applications for performing rights should be made, enclosing a reply paid envelope.

Each sketch runs for approximately eight to ten minutes.

Published by:
National Christian Education Council
Robert Denholm House
Nutfield
Redhill RH1 4HW

Published for:
RADIUS
Christ Church and Upton Chapel
Kennington Road
London SE1 7PQ

British Library Cataloguing-in-Publication Data:
A catalogue record for this book is available from the British Library.

ISBN 0-7197-0829-X

A co-operative venture in Christian Drama by NCEC and RADIUS.

Series Editors: Sylvia Read and William Fry

RADIUS is the shortened name of the Religious Drama Society of Great Britain, bringing together amateur and professional actors, writers, and others involved in religion and the performing arts.

RADIUS exists to encourage all drama which throws light on the human condition, especially through a Christian understanding. It aims to help local congregations towards a deeper appreciation of all types of drama, to inform them of opportunities to see work of a high quality, to give the technical advice and assistance needed for a good standard of local productions, and to help them find ways of introducing the lively arts into their worship.

The society runs a unique lending library, organizes an annual summer school, holds regular play-writing competitions and publishes its own magazine.

First published 1993
© Edmund Banyard 1993

All rights reserved. No part of this publication may be reproduced, stored in a retrieval system, or transmitted in any form, electronic, mechanical, photocopying, recording or other means without the prior permission of the publisher.

Typesetting by One and a Half Graphics, Redhill, Surrey
Printed by Halstan & Co Ltd, Amersham, Buckinghamshire

CONTENTS

ST BONIO'S RECEIVES A VISITOR
A SKETCH FOR FOUR PLAYERS

The Players are:-

THE VISITOR
THREE SKELETONS   THE SECRETARY
THE TREASURER
THE YOUTH LEADER

Production Note
When this was first produced at a Council for World Mission Conference at The Hayes, Swanwick, the Skeletons had simple masks and fronts down to the waist and the Secretary and Treasurer were in a bed made from two tables put together. On that occasion the sketch concluded very effectively with a dancer portraying the Holy Spirit removing the Skeleton masks from the characters and pointing them to new life.

Biblical Background
Ezekiel 37.1–14, 'Can these bones live?' The answer on that occasion was 'Yes they can'.

The SECRETARY and the TREASURER are curled up inconspicuously in bed or in sleeping bags. The YOUTH LEADER appears when she goes to answer the door. This sketch is written with the VISITOR and the YOUTH LEADER female and the SECRETARY and the TREASURER male but could easily be varied.

A bell is heard and then a voice.

VISITOR	*(Off-stage)* Is anybody there? *(After a pause and much louder)* Is – anybody – there?
SECRETARY	*(Looking up from bed)* Did you speak?
TREASURER	No.
SECRETARY	Good. *(Lies down again)*

5

The bell is rung more vigorously.

VISITOR	*(Shouting)* Where are you all? I'm your visitor, I've arrived!
SECRETARY	Is that someone at the door?
TREASURER	*(As YOUTH LEADER hurries across the stage)* She's going.
SECRETARY	That's all right then.
TREASURER	Can't think who it would be.
SECRETARY	Come to the wrong address I expect. *(Curls up again)*
VISITOR	*(Entering followed by YOUTH LEADER)* Good day to you. This is St Bonio's I trust?
TREASURER	And All Weevils.
VISITOR	I beg your pardon?
YOUTH LEADER	It's the name of the church, 'St Bonio's and All Weevils'.
VISITOR	I see. I'm glad I'm inside at last. I had some trouble making myself heard.
TREASURER	Not merely inside, Madam, you've reached the dead centre.
VISITOR	*(Slightly aggrieved)* Then could you tell the Secretary I'm here. I AM expected.
TREASURER	I'm the Treasurer. Have you come very far?
VISITOR	Yes.
TREASURER	Oh! I hope we're not responsible for your expenses.
YOUTH LEADER	This is the Secretary. *(Waking him)* Secretary, you're wanted.
SECRETARY	I'm not expecting anybody. Oh, very well. *(Sits up in bed or sleeping bag)* What's it all about?
VISITOR	Surely you received my letter?
TREASURER	As Church Secretary he's very busy, very busy indeed. It's a very responsible post. He hasn't got time to read letters.
SECRETARY	I only took it on temporarily you know, just till someone permanent could be appointed.
VISITOR	Ah, that explains it. You haven't been doing the job for long.
SECRETARY	*(Complacently)* Thirty-three years.
VISITOR	*(Almost screaming)* Thirty-three years!
TREASURER	We don't have a Church Meeting very often.
VISITOR	If it really is all that time you must have seen a good many changes.
SECRETARY	Changes?
TREASURER	*(More complacent still)* We don't hold with changes.
SECRETARY	We have appointed a Youth Leader.
YOUTH LEADER	That's me.
VISITOR	*(Hopefully)* Have you much youth work?

6

TREASURER	No.
YOUTH LEADER	We haven't really started yet, but I've got some ideas.
SECRETARY	And we altered the notice board when the new Minister came.
VISITOR	When was that?
SECRETARY	1963 was it?
TREASURER	Strange man. Wanted us to learn new hymns.
VISITOR	But you enjoyed them when you got to know them?
SECRETARY	*(Emphatically)* We never got to know them.
TREASURER	And he wanted coffee after morning service to make new people welcome.
SECRETARY	We told him, we never have new people, so what's the point?
YOUTH LEADER	*(Brightly)* I thought it might have been a good idea.
TREASURER	*(Putting her down)* Don't be stupid.
YOUTH LEADER	Sorry.
VISITOR	That's the Minister whose name is on the notice board?
SECRETARY	Yes.
VISITOR	Where does he live?
SECRETARY	Where did he go?
TREASURER	Australia, wasn't it?
VISITOR	*(Horrified)* You mean he's not Minister here now?
TREASURER	He never settled.
SECRETARY	Only stayed nine or ten years. I don't think his heart was in it.
VISITOR	*(Visibly shaken, but battling on)* Tell me, what do you do for the world outside?
SECRETARY	Outside?
TREASURER	Young woman, you have no conception of what it takes to keep St Bonio's and all Weevils open. Heating, maintenance, cleaning . . .
VISITOR	But if it's such a burden, have you thought of moving, or altering the building?
TREASURER	Altering it! A building full of history!
SECRETARY	*(Pointing)* Look, that's our family pew. Twelve seats.
VISITOR	Twelve of you?
SECRETARY	There were. I'm the only one left, but it's still our pew. No one else would think of sitting in it.
YOUTH LEADER	Of course not.
TREASURER	You've been asking a lot of questions Madam, now let me

	ask you a couple. Who sent you and why are you here?
VISITOR	The Lord sent me to prophesy.
TREASURER	Prophesy!
SECRETARY	We don't go in for that sort of thing here.
VISITOR	The Word of the Lord came to me and he showed me St Bonio's and he said, 'Woman, go prophesy to St Bonio's and cry, "Can these dry bones live?"'
TREASURER	Bones!
SECRETARY	Live! We *are* alive.
YOUTH LEADER	Are we?
TREASURER	That's enough from you.
YOUTH LEADER	Sorry.
VISITOR	And the Lord said, 'go prophesy to St Bonio's and say, "Come alive! Come alive, you walking dead. Come alive, you people without expectations. Come alive, you who have forgotten how to hope, and hear the Word of the Lord."'
SECRETARY	*(Aside, to Treasurer)* I knew it. One of these people who can't let well alone!
TREASURER	I've met your sort before. Next thing we know you'll be wanting us to get involved with people outside the church!
SECRETARY	I've better things to do than listen to you. *(Gets back to sleep)*
TREASURER	The Youth Leader will show you out. *(Also gets back to sleep)*
VISITOR	Oh St Bonio's, St Bonio's!
TREASURER	*(Looking up)* 'And All Weevils' if you don't mind. *(He lies down again)*
YOUTH LEADER	It's no good, you'll not wake them now. You are quite right, we are dead. St Bonio's is finished.
VISITOR	That wasn't my message.
YOUTH LEADER	But we're nothing but skeletons.
VISITOR	You may think and behave like skeletons, but peel it off and there is a living person underneath.
YOUTH LEADER	Peel it off? It sounds painful.
VISITOR	Maybe, but if you start thinking you're alive, behaving as though you are alive, you'll soon find you really *are* alive.
YOUTH LEADER	But I'm nobody. I couldn't change anything.
VISITOR	Couldn't you?
YOUTH LEADER	*(Wistfully)* I wish . . .
VISITOR	Yes?

YOUTH LEADER	*(Her face falls again)* It's no good.
VISITOR	If you'd like we could keep in touch. Between us . . . who knows?
YOUTH LEADER	I wouldn't mind that.
VISITOR	That's it then, we'll make something of St Bonio's yet. You'll see. *(They go)*
TREASURER	*(Looking up again)* Has she gone?
SECRETARY	Yes, I think so.
TREASURER	We don't want any more visitors like that.
SECRETARY	No, but what can we do about it?
TREASURER	We could get rid of the bell.
SECRETARY	Good idea. *(After pause)* I say.
TREASURER	Yes?
SECRETAR	Who do you think REALLY sent her?
TREASURER	God knows!
SECRETARY	Sleep well.
TREASURER	You too. Good night.

Talking Point

Of course the situation portrayed here is absurd and the audience are meant to laugh at the exaggeration, but is there an underlying truth we may need to face? Could those performing and watching themselves be shutting eyes and ears to what God would have them be doing? Might there be ways in which even they need to hear the call to 'Come alive'?

THE SLEEPING BEAUTY OF FLEET STREET
A FABLE FOR THREE VOICES

Production Note
This can be presented without any special furniture, but careful attention still needs to be paid to the acting area to make sure that the three players can be seen and heard and that they can move freely. Do bring out the contrast between the occasions when they are addressing the audience and those when they are addressing each other.

Biblical Background
John 14.6, 'I am the way, the truth and the life.' Many other Gospel passages are appropriate e.g. Matthew 6.25−34, 'Surely life is more than food, the body more than clothes.'

The three VOICES are each addressing the audience except on those occasions when they are quite obviously talking to one another. The difference needs to be brought out in the production.

VOICE 1	Once upon a time . . .
VOICE 2	*(Who rather likes correcting other people)* And not so very long ago, in fact, quite recently.
VOICE 1	In the centre of London . . .
VOICE 2	In Fleet Street. *(To ONE)* It was in Fleet Street, you might as well be precise . . .
VOICE 1	Very well, in Fleet Street, a large office block, built of steel and glass and concrete was being demolished . . .
VOICE 2	. . . To make room for an even larger office block of concrete, steel and glass.
VOICE 1	As they were intending to build higher than ever before . . .
VOICE 2	Oh, much, much, MUCH higher; higher even than Canary Wharf . . .

VOICE 1	They had to excavate deeper than ever before.
VOICE 2	Much, MUCH deeper, down below the sub-soil; right down into the sub-sub-SUB soil.
VOICE 1	Suddenly the workmen broke into an underground chamber where a girl lay in a deep sleep.
VOICE 2	*(Breaking the mood)* She'd missed the last train.
VOICE 1	*(Slightly annoyed, to TWO)* What d'you mean, she'd missed the last train?
VOICE 2	On the Underground.
VOICE 1	Nothing to do with trains. She had come from another age, another time.
VOICE 2	She got left behind from a Dr Who series?
VOICE 1	It's nothing to do with Dr Who.
VOICE 2	Go on then, I'll buy it; how did she get there?
VOICE 1	*(Addressing the audience again)* No one knew; and they didn't know where she'd come from, or how long she'd been there; but when the light broke in she came to life. They brought her out and she looked about her as though she was seeing the world for the very first time.
VOICE 2	What rotten luck!
VOICE 1	*(Puzzled, to TWO)* What d'you you mean, 'What rotten luck!'?
VOICE 2	*(To audience)* The first thing she ever sees of the world, and it's a building site in Fleet Street.
VOICE 1	*(To TWO)* Maybe, maybe not. *(To audience again)* The site belonged to a famous daily newspaper which had moved away . . .
VOICE 2	*(Breaking in)* I see! The paper naturally scooped the story. 'Sensational, exclusive! Read the amazing account of the Sleeping Beauty of Fleet Street.'
VOICE 1	Well. Yes, it was a bit like that. The owner of the paper . . .
VOICE 2	*(Breaking in again)* With that sense of what the great British public wants which had made him a multi-millionaire . . .
VOICE 1	*(Regaining the initiative)* Decided to take up the story of this mysterious girl and arranged to interview her himself that very afternoon.
VOICE 2	No journalist?
VOICE 1	*(To TWO)* He had a journalist there to write the copy.
VOICE 2	That figures.
VOICE 1	*(To audience again)* He found her very sweet and very grateful for all that was being done for her . . .
VOICE 2	From which he was going to make a packet . . .

VOICE 1	But he learned nothing of where she had come from and when he asked her what she wanted most the only answer he got was . . .
VOICE 3	*(Who has just entered from behind the others adopts a meek sweet voice to say −)* I want to learn how to live.
VOICE 2	*(Not over pleased)* Are you playing the girl?
VOICE 3	*(In a very different tone)* Any objections?
VOICE 2	She's supposed to be a sweet-natured beauty.
VOICE 3	So what! If you're suggesting that I'm not sweet-natured and beautiful . . .
VOICE 1	I think perhaps we ought to continue.
VOICE 2	Sure, don't mind me.
VOICE 3	*(Emphatically)* I mind!
VOICE 1	*(Bravely returning to addressing the audience)* The newspaper owner explained that if she wanted to learn how to live she couldn't have woken up at a better time or place. Nobody in the whole world knew more about living than the folks who spent their lives producing his newspaper.
VOICE 2	That's one way of looking at it
VOICE 1	This was the beginning of a story that featured prominently in that paper for the next six weeks.

> *During the following speeches VOICES 1 & 2 show rising excitement, but VOICE 3 keeps to a matter of fact way of speaking.*

VOICE 2	Six weeks! That's fantastic!
VOICE 1	It was a fantastic story. Everything possible was done so that this girl might live as no-one had ever lived before . . .
VOICE 2	And every experience, every lavish treat, was of course faithfully and exclusively recorded and published for the delight of the great British public.
VOICE 3	There was a suite at the Hilton. Charming escorts to the many events it was imagined that no one who wanted to live would dream of missing . . .
VOICE 2	The accumulated wisdom of the paper's readers was harnessed through competitions so that no stimulus to living might be overlooked.
VOICE 1	And so the 'Sleeping Beauty of Fleet Street' who had woken so suddenly and surprisingly to the modern world was taken to . . .
VOICE 3	*(She is reciting a list, but without any great enthusiasm)* Operas, theatres, night clubs, lunches, dinners, the Boat Race, the Cup

	Final, Henley, Wimbledon, museums, art galleries, National Trust houses, English Heritage castles . . .
VOICE 1	She had a song written for her which went to the top of the charts and she appeared on every television channel in turn. She went shopping at . . .
VOICE 3	*(Continuing)* Harrods, John Lewis's, Marks and Spencer's, Asda, Tesco's, Sainsbury's, Selfridges . . .
VOICE 2	All right, all right, you've made your point.
VOICE 1	During all this time she was dressed by the most fashionable houses, ate in the most exclusive restaurants . . .
VOICE 2	And met all the people who thought they mattered.
VOICE 1	She even had lunch with the Prime Minister.
VOICE 2	Big deal.
VOICE 3	But at the end of the sixth week she was very tired and was taken to a leading doctor . . .
VOICE 2	Who of course prescribed the very latest in pep-pills.
VOICE 3	She asked for some time without any engagements and so for a whole day she was left to herself.
VOICE 2	Think of that, a whole day!
VOICE 3	It happened to be a Sunday, which is a very dead day in central London. There was the luxury of a late breakfast, and then a stroll out into the near deserted streets. With nothing particular in mind she looked to see if any buildings were open, and so by chance dropped in on two different church services.
VOICE 1	At the time she didn't realise what they were.
VOICE 2	As there hadn't been any fashionable weddings, state funerals, coronations or anything of that sort, attending church hadn't figured in her programme.
VOICE 3	The services seemed a little gloomy and not very popular, but there was something that caught her attention, particularly one phrase, 'I am the way, the truth, and the life'. Again and again that day it came back to her, together with one or two other words that had been read about the man who had said it.
VOICE 1	Next day she was scheduled to have lunch with the newspaper proprietor to talk over her future.
VOICE 2	He had great news for her. He had arranged an advertising contract with a mattress manufacturer who wanted to run a great sales drive under the slogan, 'You too could sleep through the centuries'.
VOICE 1	But even when he named the fee that had been agreed she seemed strangely inattentive. Eventually she broke in to what he was saying . . .

13

VOICE 3	What does it all mean? What does all this activity add up to? What's the point of all I've been doing? What I want to do is to learn how to live.
VOICE 1	But this is living, he cried.
VOICE 2	She told him how she had wandered into the two churches . . .
VOICE 3	I felt when I was there that there could be something else to life if only I could find it.
VOICE 1	He was greatly concerned and offered her an appointment with his own psychiatrist.
VOICE 2	He couldn't have been kinder.
VOICE 1	She didn't reply to his offer, she just said.
VOICE 3	Thank you for the lunch and for all you have done for me in these last weeks.
VOICE 1	She left him there, and nobody ever saw her again.
VOICE 2	Had she taken anything from her hotel suite?
VOICE 3	Just a few simple clothes and a little money.
VOICE 2	*(To ONE)* There was that late night reveller who said he'd seen her go down into the foundations of a new building and disappear.
VOICE 1	Rubbish.
VOICE 3	There's another possibility.
VOICE 1	What's that?
VOICE 3	About that time a girl who wouldn't talk about her past found a room in a back street in Birmingham and took a job in a snack bar. When things weren't too busy you'd find her talking with people about what it means to be alive.
VOICE 2	*(They are now talking to each other again)* Where is she now?
VOICE 3	What does it matter?
VOICE 2	True. What does it matter. Why are we telling this silly story anyway?
VOICE 1	Maybe it isn't so silly.
VOICE 3	When the Sleeping Beauty of Fleet Street said, 'I want to learn how to live,' didn't she speak for every one of us?
VOICE 2	What are you getting at?
VOICE 1	She was shown one way and she didn't think much of it.
VOICE 2	You're not suggesting that a back street in Birmingham is better than a suite at the Hilton are you?
VOICE 3	Maybe, maybe not. It depends where it leads, which way it's going.
VOICE 2	Which way? What way?
VOICE 1	I get what she means. You're thinking of 'I am the way, the truth, and the life.'

VOICE 2	Is that what you mean?
VOICE 3	Yes, I suppose I do.
VOICE 2	I thought we'd have to finish up with a moral.
VOICE 1	Why shouldn't we finish up with a moral?
VOICE 3	It's not really a moral is it? It's more a question.
VOICE 2	All right, I'll buy it; what's the question?
VOICE 3	Is life, real life, a matter of taking all you can get or, well, is it something else? It's as simple as that.
VOICE 1	Simple?
VOICE 3	Yes simple. Of course there's nowhere it says that the simple is easy.
VOICE 2	Ummm! I'll think about it.
VOICE 3	Why don't we all do just that?
VOICE 2	*(As they go)* I didn't mean I'd think SERIOUSLY about it.
VOICE 1	Why not?
VOICE 3	Yes, why not?
VOICE 2	Well, to begin with, if I'd been her I'd have stuck with the suite at the Hilton . . .

They have now disappeared, presumably still arguing.

Talking Point

This fable poses the question 'Where do we find life?' Is it fair to suggest that the churches the girl visited were dull? Anyway what was wrong with the 'life' she was offered? Is Christianity a matter of giving up pleasant things or might it be seen as offering a new focus for life which places a different value on all things?

THE TWO SONS
A STORY FOR THREE VOICES

Production Note
This can be presented without any special furniture. Although certain passages are addressed directly to the audience the three characters are quite distinctive and the characterization should be maintained throughout.

Biblical Background
Matthew 21.28−32, The parable of the two sons.

VOICE 1 is the NARRATOR and also the FATHER, VOICE 2 is the MOTHER and VOICE 3 is ANDY.

VOICE 1   This is a story of two teenage brothers. The first is called Algernon . . .

VOICE 2   *(Breaking in with all the pride of a fond mother)* Oh he's such a dear boy, you really would like my Algernon; so polite and such charming manners. He takes a real pride in his appearance; he's always neat and tidy and what's more, I've never known him slam a door or leave a mess behind him. Believe me, it's a pleasure to have him around the house.

VOICE 3   *(With feeling)* Little creep!

VOICE 2   *(Angrily)* What did you say?

VOICE 3   I said he's a little creep!

VOICE 2   *(Claiming the high moral ground)* Andy, that's no way to speak of your brother. I only wish you could be a little more like him. Yes I do; and it's not just me; Mrs Davis notices it . . .

VOICE 3   *(Breaking in angrily)* Trust you to listen to that bitchy old scandalmonger, there's nothing she ever misses . . .

VOICE 2   *(Indignantly)* Andy! Mrs Davis is a very knowledgeable woman and highly respected.

VOICE 3   Who by?

16

VOICE 2	*(Ignoring the interruption)* Only yesterday she said to me, 'It's a great pity that your Andy can't be a little bit more like his brother Algernon.'
VOICE 3	And you pay attention to the silly old . . .
VOICE 2	Andy!
VOICE 3	I give up. *(They glare at one another)*
VOICE 1	*(Who has been keeping in the background comes forward to speak to the audience again)* Andy, you must understand, is a constant source of worry to his mother. I have to admit that his things are all over the house and it's no pleasure to eat with him. Something is sure to be knocked over as he reaches across the table; you just hope it won't land in your lap . . .
VOICE 2	*(Who has turned away from Andy to listen)* That isn't the half of it; look at the language he uses, I don't know where he gets it from, he's never learnt it in this house: and all that pop music blaring out wherever he goes, and his hair cut . . .
VOICE 1	*(Patiently)* You're quite right, my dear.
VOICE 2	*(Not to be stopped)* I know I am. And just look at the state of his clothes. I wash and iron for him just the same as I do for the rest of you but you'd never think it. He goes around looking as though he's wearing Oxfam rejects.
VOICE 1	Yes dear, I know. *(To audience)* So you see there's a bit of a problem. However, to come to the matter I want to share with you. Last Saturday I'd got quite a lot to get through, so I said to Algy and Andy, 'Would one of you two lads be good enough to give the car a clean this morning?' I suppose I should have expected Andy's response.
VOICE 3	You can stick that for a lark. I've done more than my share of cleaning that car. Anyway I told Dick I'd go with him to get a new bike.
VOICE 2	*(Andy has condemned himself)* Algernon wouldn't speak like that.
VOICE 1	No, no, he wouldn't, I quite agree. *(Turning to audience again)* Andy went off, I heard the door slam behind him, but Algernon said, 'Of course I'll do it Dad, leave it to me.'
VOICE 2	Exactly, you know as well as I do, you can always count on my Algernon.
VOICE 1	Nothing happened for a while.
VOICE 2	*(Jumping to Algernon's defence)* You didn't expect him to run out straight away did you? He's got other things to do and you weren't in a hurry for it.

VOICE 1	No, I wasn't in a hurry, but at lunch time the car still hadn't been cleaned. It was mid-afternoon when I at last heard someone at work on it.
VOICE 2	*(With mother's pride)* And a very good job Algernon made of it. I remember thinking how clean the car looked on Sunday. It was an absolute picture.
VOICE 1	You're quite right, my dear, it did, only it wasn't Algernon who cleaned it, it was Andy.
VOICE 2	*(Disbelieving)* You're joking!
VOICE 1	He never said anything, and if I hadn't looked out of the window I might not have known; but it was Andy who actually did the job.
VOICE 3	*(To audience, almost apologetically)* There's no need to look at me like that. Well, when I got back it was standing there, and anyway, I hadn't got anything else to do. *(With a hint of aggression)* You needn't think I'm a soft touch . . .
VOICE 1	*(To VOICE 2)* Well?
VOICE 2	Mrs Davis'll never believe it. *(She finds it hard to believe it herself)*
VOICE 3	Mrs Davis can go to . . .
VOICE 2	*(Outraged)* Andy!
VOICE 3	*(After the slightest of pauses)* . . . Bognor.
VOICE 1	*(To audience)* It was Jesus who told that story.
VOICE 2	*(Seeing a way to hit back)* I don't remember any story in the Bible about cleaning cars.
VOICE 1	No my dear, of course not; the story Jesus told was about working in a Vineyard, but the point was the same.
VOICE 2	*(She never gives up)* Well, I don't know, I don't think you ought to change Bible stories like that; Algernon would probably have enjoyed working in a vineyard. Anyway, I'm sure Jesus would want us to be polite and tidy, and careful about how we speak.
VOICE 1	Yes, but he did make the point that much more important than saying the right things is actually doing them.
VOICE 2	*(She is never disadvantaged for long)* That reminds me; Mrs Davis wants her hedge cut.
VOICE 3	*(To audience)* Mrs Davis! I'm off! *(He goes)*
VOICE 1	We'll have to see what we can do.
VOICE 2	*(As they exit)* I still say that you ought to be careful how you speak and that you should always be neat and tidy, especially when you go to church. It's not only Mrs Davis who notices . . .
VOICE 1	*(Who has learned over the years that the soft answer turneth away wrath)* Yes, my dear, yes, yes, you're quite right . . .

Talking Point

This is a straightforward adaptation of a parable into a modern situation. As originally told it was good 'religious' people who were portrayed as saying the right things but not doing them and people outside the church who actually did what the Father wanted. Are there any uncomfortable parallels in the life we know today?

THE SHREWD AND THE SIMPLE
A SKETCH FOR FIVE PLAYERS

Production Note
A table and five chairs are all the furniture required; it is not the sort of meeting where people keep minutes, even if they really ought to do so.

Biblical Background
Luke 16.1−8, The parable of the dishonest steward.

We are listening in on the meeting of an ad hoc committee as they settle around a table.

TONY	Are we all here?
MADGE	John said he was coming.
TONY	*(A little anxiously)* Oh dear, I do hope − I mean, he's a decent enough fellow, but he does have some very strange ideas.
CYRIL	*(Confidently)* Don't worry Tony: when he's been with us a bit longer, he'll get used to our ways.
MARY	*(Who feels John has a mind of his own)* I doubt it.
CYRIL	Well, I hope he will anyway.
MADGE	*(Eager to pass on her news)* Have you heard about the trouble with his business?
TONY	No, what's happened?
MADGE	I'm told one of his managers has gone off with the firm's money.
CYRIL	*(Always in the know)* Yes, I heard that today. Something like a hundred thousand pounds I was told.
TONY	A hundred thousand! That'll set him back a bit.
MARY	*(Concerned)* Will they have to close?
CYRIL	No, they're big enough to weather it. But it'll be a blow; he must be hopping mad.
MARY	And he's such a hard working man himself.
TONY	And straight. I'll say that for him.

MADGE	That sounds like him coming now. *(As JOHN enters)* Hullo John.
JOHN	*(Taking off his coat and making for a vacant chair)* Evening all. Hope I haven't kept you waiting.
MADGE	No, we were here early.
MARY	We're sorry to hear about your firm. *(And she is)*
JOHN	The firm? Oh, you've heard about our spot of trouble.
CYRIL	*(Eager to confirm the details)* Sounds a nasty business. Is it true that a hundred thousand has gone?
JOHN	Probably more. It'll take some time to sort out. I wasn't too pleased about it, I can tell you, but it's all water under the bridge now. Anyway, what have we got to discuss tonight?
MADGE	The rain's coming in again.
MARY	*(Who is a caring soul)* Last Sunday morning when we had that shower in the middle of service some fell right on Mrs Evans.
TONY	*(Who only ever sees the short term solutions)* We've warned her before, but she won't sit in another pew.
JOHN	So what are you suggesting Tony?
TONY	It looks as though we'll have to get the builders to look at that end of the roof again. I don't see what else we *can* do.
CYRIL	*(Almost as if it were an achievement)* We've spent a small fortune on that roof in the last few years.
JOHN	And not only the roof I fancy.
CYRIL	Yes. There were those window frames of course.
MADGE	And there's more will need doing soon; have you noticed the draught when the wind is in the east?
MARY	The floor where we sit is in a bad state.
CYRIL	*(As one who knows every last woodworm personally)* The floor's in a bad state everywhere.
TONY	Oh, I don't know about that.
MADGE	I do!
JOHN	I know I'm a newcomer to this group, but I've been in the church six years now and it's the same tale all the time. Mend a bit here, patch a bit there; year after year pouring out money on a building that has outlived its usefulness.
TONY	*(Horrified)* Outlived its usefulness?
JOHN	Certainly! It's run down, out of date, expensive to operate, and three quarters of the space is hardly ever used.
TONY	*(Anxious to get back to the comfortable familiarity of the business they are always discussing)* Aren't we getting away from the point? We only came to talk about that bit of roof.

MARY	*(Asking a serious question)* John, you're not suggesting that we should pull the whole place down and start again, are you?
JOHN	Yes Mary, I suppose I am, that, or a complete reconstruction.
MARY	*(Fearful of such radical suggestions)* The older members of the congregation wouldn't like that.
JOHN	How do you know they wouldn't until you ask them? You might get a surprise.
TONY	And where would the money come from?
JOHN	Where does the money come from that we spend year after year on short term repairs?
MARY	*(Quite sincerely)* We pray about it and it comes.
MADGE	*(The practical one)* People are very good. There's fund-raising all year round.
JOHN	Then don't you think people might rise to a new and imaginative redevelopment scheme if it were put to them?
CYRIL	That would want a lot of thinking about. *(Meaning he doesn't want to think about it at all)*
TONY	*(He's out of his depth and anxious to get back to where his feet touch bottom)* We really ought to get back to the matter of the repairs to the roof.
MADGE	*(Eager to get things settled and be off)* Yes, I can't stay much longer.
CYRIL	*(To finish off John's suggestion once and for all)* I know there are places where redevelopment has worked, but I wouldn't have thought it would be right for us here.
MARY	*(In all sincerity)* Don't you think we're meant to do the little things that come to us day by day and leave the rest with the Lord?
JOHN	If you mean that we should never take a long view of things, never really look ahead, no, I don't. When I came in you were talking about the manager I've just lost. Did any of you know him?
OTHERS	No . . . Never met him . . . *(etc.)*
JOHN	Then let me tell you something about him. He was with us on a three year contract and I'd given him good warning that it was unlikely to be renewed. From that moment, so I've since learned, he skilfully diverted company money into his own pocket. He's now settled in sunny Spain, out of our reach, with enough to keep him for the rest of his life.
MARY	*(Genuinely sorry)* That really is awful.
CYRIL	*(Saying the right thing)* Yes, we're all deeply sorry for you John.
MADGE	*(Who probably doesn't trust too many people anyway)* To have trusted a man and been let down in that way.

TONY	*(Meaning it)* You deserve better than that.
JOHN	He did the dirty on me and there's no doubt he's left a good old mess behind him. But there's one thing I give him credit for, however reluctantly.
MADGE	*(In amazement)* Give him credit!
JOHN	Yes, and I'll tell you why; he realised that he was faced with a crisis and he made plans to meet it. Naturally I don't agree with his solution, you'd hardly expect me to, but at least he found one.
TONY	I don't understand you. *(He's not the only one)*
MARY	What on earth do you mean.
JOHN	Look, you are dear people and you're as honest as the day is long, but you can't see that you're facing a crisis that calls for decisive and imaginative action.
TONY	*(Clinging to what he can understand)* We're only here to talk about putting a few tiles back on the roof.
JOHN	*(Making his point forcefully but with complete good humour)* Exactly! And that's what's wrong. Try thinking about the rogue who swindled me. There's something you could learn from him. Better still have a look . . . *(Bringing out a pocket book)* . . . I made a note of it somewhere . . . yes, this is it, Luke sixteen, particularly notice verse eight. I'm sorry, I must be off. Let me know if you want to look further into the question of redevelopment. I've got one or two ideas. *(He goes)*
CYRIL	*(Dismissing the subject)* He's a strange chap is John.
MADGE	Fancy suggesting we could learn something from a criminal.
TONY	*(Getting a Bible)* Luke sixteen did he say? Ah, I've got it. *(He reads to himself for a moment then says in a puzzled tone)* It's the parable of the dishonest steward.
MARY	And what is verse eight all about?
TONY	*(Reading it carefully)* 'The master commended the dishonest steward for his prudence; for the sons of this world are wiser in their own generation than the sons of light.'
MADGE	I never did understand that.
CYRIL	*(The first attempt to dismiss John's ideas having failed he comes in with the heavy artillery)* This is no time for reading the Bible, we've got a practical matter to settle. D'you think we could get back to the subject?
MARY	What are we going to do about the roof then?
TONY	Shall I get the builder round to patch up that corner?
OTHERS	Yes . . . good idea . . . *(etc.)*

TONY   *(As they go)* Sorry we wasted so much time, but you know what John is . . . *(The rest make general murmurs of agreement)*

Talking Point

This parable has always presented difficulties. Why should a crook be commended for his dishonesty?

The sketch seeks to bring out what the author believes to be the parable's meaning. Do you agree that it is not enough to be 'nice'? That refusal to face up to major problems or challenges turns niceness into ineffectiveness? Can you apply this to any situation you know?

A NEW CREATION
A DIALOGUE FOR FIVE VOICES

Production Note
To bring the best out of this dialogue particular care needs to be taken over placing, and moving, the five characters in your acting area.

Biblical Background
2 Corinthians 5.17−21, Revelation 21.1−5.

Verse
'Just as I am' Charlotte Elliot 1789−1871.

The READER is sitting centrally turning over the pages of a Bible and when reading aloud, he/she does so as one who is making fresh discoveries. The two couples are seated either side of the READER with a little distance between each group. All except the READER are, to begin with, glancing at newspapers or magazines. The FIRST MAN and FIRST WOMAN are the younger couple. There is a noticeable change of mood as the dialogue progresses. At the end the three groups have become one.

READER	Listen to this, 'The One who sat on the throne said, "I am making all things new".'
FIRST MAN	Then for starters I'll have a new car.
SECOND MAN	*(Calling across to him)* Trouble with yours old chap?
FIRST MAN	You can say that again. Never anything else.
FIRST WOMAN	*(Dreaming aloud)* A new outfit, that's what I need. I've nothing decent to wear.
FIRST MAN	Wouldn't it be better to wait till the spring?
FIRST WOMAN	Just like a man. 'Wait till the spring.' I'll need another one then, stupid.
SECOND WOMAN	*(Sadly)* In our house everything seems to be wearing out at once. Even the telly's gone on the blink.
SECOND MAN	The telly! I didn't realise! That's serious. We'll have to get

25

	a new one straight away. There are some good offers if you shop around.
FIRST MAN	*(Calling across)* Make sure you get a video with it.
FIRST WOMAN	Haven't you got a video?
SECOND WOMAN	What would I do with a video?
FIRST WOMAN	Record programmes and see them later.
SECOND WOMAN	But I watch all the time anyway. I'll have to think about it. I don't know about the money though, we've just had a new kitchen fitted.
SECOND MAN	No problem. We'll use our credit card.
FIRST MAN	If you've got a video you don't need to watch all those miserable current affairs programmes.
SECOND WOMAN	I don't watch them anyway.
FIRST WOMAN	Of course not. You want to forget what's going on in the world, not be reminded of it.
READER	*(The Reader has continued reading and now stands and slowly reads aloud; for the moment the others are forgotten)* 'I saw a new heaven and a new earth, for the first heaven and the first earth had vanished.'
SECOND WOMAN	*(Thoughtfully)* A new earth maybe, but why a new heaven?
FIRST MAN	*(Over brightly)* Been mucked up by all that space junk flying around.
FIRST WOMAN	Don't be silly.
SECOND WOMAN	It's a lovely dream.
FIRST WOMAN	What is?
SECOND WOMAN	To be able to make a new start.
SECOND MAN	What sort of new start?
SECOND WOMAN	Well, no more unemployment, or people sleeping on the streets . . .
FIRST MAN	*(Joining in quite seriously)* No more pollution, or nuclear waste . . .
SECOND MAN	You could go on *ad infinitum* — no more violence, no more stockpiling of armaments. But what's the use of dreaming?
FIRST WOMAN	You're right. It's always been like this hasn't it? You can't change things now.
SECOND MAN	No. Where's a new earth going to come from? You can't trade-in the old one.
READER	'For anyone united to Christ there is a new creation: the old order has gone, a new order has already begun.'

SECOND MAN	*(Getting up and going across to the READER)* What have you got there? *(Looking over his shoulder)* Oh, it's a Bible. Why do people always have to bring religion in?
FIRST WOMAN	They do it at Christmas, too.
SECOND MAN	Do what?
FIRST WOMAN	Bring religion in.
SECOND MAN	You can't get away from it.
SECOND WOMAN	*(Getting up and joining SECOND MAN and the READER)* I've nothing against religion, *(Wistfully)* if only God weren't so far away.
SECOND MAN	*(Very down to earth)* No, I've nothing against religion for them that want it; but we've got to live in this world, not dream about another one.
READER	It says here, 'God was in Christ reconciling the world to himself.'
SECOND MAN	And what d'you think that's supposed to mean?
SECOND WOMAN	*(Tentatively)* Making us his friends. Would that be it?
SECOND MAN	*(Indignant)* If God is so wonderful and friendly why have we got racism, terrorism, inner cities falling to pieces . . .

More indignation builds up during the next two speeches.

FIRST MAN	*(Joining in)* . . . wars, famine, disease . . .
FIRST WOMAN	. . . wife battering, child abuse . . . God! When you stop to think of it, what a mess the world is in.
SECOND WOMAN	*(She is struck by a new thought)* You know, when you do stop to think of what the world's really like, I mean, what we've done to it, how could God possibly be interested in us?
READER	*(Warming to his subject)* It goes on like this. 'God was in Christ reconciling the world to himself, no longer holding people's misdeeds against them, and he has entrusted us with the message of reconciliation.'
SECOND MAN	He's done WHAT?
FIRST MAN	*(Getting up and joining the others)* Entrusted US?
FIRST WOMAN	*(Also getting up)* Not ME, that's for sure. Nobody's ever trusted me with anything that matters.
SECOND WOMAN	I don't think I could be a messenger . . . not of a NEW world. I'm too much a part of the old one.
SECOND MAN	I guess that goes for all of us.

FIRST MAN	*(A new thought)* If we're honest, we're part of the world's mess, and it's a part of us.
READER	*(He is making a new discovery)* What about this, 'For anyone united to Christ, there is a new creation, the old order has gone, a new order has already begun.'
SECOND MAN	Already begun, a new creation? *(He can't believe this)*
FIRST MAN	A new order of things? *(Echoing SECOND MAN's disbelief)*
SECOND WOMAN	It seems to suggest that it starts just where we are.
FIRST WOMAN	D'you think it could really happen?
READER	'All this has been the work of God. He has enlisted us in this service of reconciliation.' You see, it brings us in again.
SECOND WOMAN	*(Eagerly)* I'd like to see a new world, where no one is left to cope with pain or sorrow or loneliness or anything else on their own.
SECOND MAN	*(Catching SECOND WOMAN's enthusiasm)* Where there's a passion for justice and truth and all human beings are valued for what they are in themselves.
FIRST MAN	*(Slightly reluctantly)* Yes, I suppose deep down, I'd like to see a new world where we're no longer thinking how quickly we can get our snouts in the trough.
FIRST WOMAN	*(Following FIRST MAN's mood, but growing in hope)* I've never really thought about it, not properly, but I wouldn't mind learning where to start.
READER	*(He is sharing his discovery, not lecturing the others)* I think it means that we have to start where we are. Ask God to use us as agents of his new creation. If Christ died so that we should stop living just for ourselves, maybe what we have to do is let ourselves go.
SECOND MAN	Easier said than done.

After a short pause they speak very simply in what effectively is a prayer.

FIRST WOMAN	Just as I am, without one plea But that Thy blood was shed for me, And that Thou bid'st me come to Thee, O Lamb of God, I come.
SECOND MAN	Just as I am, though tossed about

	With many a conflict, many a doubt —
FIRST MAN	Fightings and fears within, without,
BOTH MEN	O Lamb of God, I come.
SECOND WOMAN	Just as I am, poor, wretched, blind;
	Sight, riches, healing of the mind,
	Yea, all I need, in Thee to find,
ALL	O Lamb of God, we come.

Talking Point

The first reaction of the characters in the dialogue to a 'new creation' is completely materialistic. What do you think is the relation between material and spiritual? Are they entirely separate or are they interrelated? If God calls us into partnership, what might God be looking to you to be doing?

TRAVEL AGENCY
A SKETCH FOR FOUR PLAYERS

The Players are:-

TWO REPRESENTATIVES OF 'MAMMON TOURS'
A TRAVELLER
A COURIER FOR 'KINGDOM' TRAVEL

Production Note
Dress the agents for 'Mammon Tours' smartly, with the suggestion of a uniform (similar jackets), and perhaps a sash reading 'Mammon Tours'. You will need a large kit-bag, trolley and bulky parcels. The narrow entrance doesn't have to be elaborate, it need be no more than the gap between two tables close together, although a small doorway would be even more effective.

Biblical Background
Mark 10.23−27, The eye of the needle; Matthew 6.25−34, Don't be anxious − and many other passages warning of the snares of the tempter.

The two representatives of Mammon Tours enter with their bright sales patter.

MAMMON 1	Are you feeling fed-up, frustrated, fractious, frayed round the edges?
MAMMON 2	Do you want to go places − get away from it all?
MAMMON 1	Have you ever dreamt of a whole exciting new way of living?
MAMMON 2	Then book now for adventure, travel with Mammon Tours!
MAMMON 1	Mammon Tours! The agency that can take you anywhere − and beyond!
MAMMON 2	Mammon Tours! The agency that can offer you everything − and more!
MAMMON 1	Mammon Tours! The agency where you don't have to bother about the price.
MAMMON 2	Just book now − and pay later.

A TRAVELLER enters. She is unsophisticated and is both scared and fascinated by the offers made to her.

MAMMON 1	Good morning Madam! May we have the pleasure of arranging an adventure travel programme for you?
MAMMON 2	How about our special 'World of Fantasy' tour?
MAMMON 1	We can soon get you riding high!
MAMMON 2	Your feet won't touch the ground!
MAMMON 1	Reality will just fade away when you visit Dreamland!
MAMMON 2	Book now with Mammon Tours!
TRAVELLER	No, I don't think so, thank you very much.
MAMMON 1	Then what about an educational trip?
MAMMON 2	Learn how to climb on other people's backs!
MAMMON 1	Learn how to stick your elbow in someone else's eye!
MAMMON 2	Learn how to get your foot in the door and keep other people out!
TRAVELLER	I don't . . .
MAMMON 1	Why not take our specially recommended Ego-trip?
TRAVELLER	No, really, thank you very much.
MAMMON 2	No? Then the thing for you is one of our super-duper luxury cruises.
MAMMON 1	Let Mammon Tours spoil you as you've never been spoilt before.
MAMMON 2	You needn't have a care in the world. Let other people do the worrying for you.
TRAVELLER	No, no, thank you very much. You see, I know where I want to go; I've already booked with Kingdom Travel.
MAMMON 1	Kingdom Travel!
MAMMON 2	Kingdom Travel!
MAMMON 1	Madam! − I wouldn't say anything against Kingdom Travel . . .
MAMMON 2	Of course not, that would be completely unethical.
MAMMON 1	But they've been offering the same old stuff ever since the time of Noah.
MAMMON 2	In fact we can probably guess the very tour you've booked.
TRAVELLER	I . . .
MAMMON 1	No, don't tell us it's the 'Way of Life'.
MAMMON 2	You haven't booked for the 'Way of Life' trip have you?
TRAVELLER	Well . . .
MAMMON 1	She HAS, you know.
MAMMON 2	One born every minute.

MAMMON 1	I suppose it's too late, Madam, to suggest a change of plan? *(Dropping sales patter and beginning to sound plausible)*
TRAVELLER	Yes, I've quite made up my mind, I really do want to go.
MAMMON 2	Madam is quite free to make her own choice of course. *(Sounding plausible too)*
MAMMON 1	But if we could offer just one small word of disinterested advice . . .
MAMMON 2	You see we've been in this business for years and years . . .
MAMMON 1	Every bit as long as Kingdom Travel . . .
MAMMON 2	Only we move with the times.
MAMMON 1	I can't help noticing that you've hardly got any luggage.
TRAVELLER	But, I understood that I didn't need much luggage, I thought . . . *(She is beginning to trust them)*
MAMMON 2	*(Aside to MAMMON 1)* She thought!
MAMMON 1	It's always the same with Kingdom Travel. No glossy brochures; no detailed instructions. You could turn up in the noddy as far as THEY'RE concerned.
TRAVELLER	Well, I did just wonder . . . *(She is wavering)*
MAMMON 1	Quite.
MAMMON 2	Who wouldn't wonder.
MAMMON 1	*(Very kind and helpful)* Say no more. Just let us kit you out.
MAMMON 2	*(Eagerly)* We're used to rush jobs.
TRAVELLER	But how do I pay? *(They have won her over)*
MAMMON 1	Don't think about that now. Just pay as you go along.
MAMMON 2	You need to cut a decent figure among your fellow passengers don't you think? Why, you never know who might be there.
TRAVELLER	*(Wavering again)* If you're really sure?
MAMMON 1	Of course we are sure.
MAMMON 2	You can trust us.
MAMMON 1	First of all you will need this. *(Provides a large kit bag)*
MAMMON 2	And this. *(Provides a large trolley)*
MAMMON 1	Now we will start loading you up.

Between them the two AGENTS load the TRAVELLER with parcels. These should be bulky and clearly labelled. Choose your own labels, some possibilities are: Pride, Envy, Greed, Selfishness, Ambition, Clothes, Make-up, Property, Investments, Social Status, . . . As they load the parcels the AGENTS say clearly what they are.

MAMMON 1	*(When they have finished)* That looks more like it!

MAMMON 2	With that you ought to be able to enjoy yourself, even with Kingdom Travel.
	The COURIER enters.
COURIER	*(To TRAVELLER)* Hullo! I'm your Courier. Welcome to Kingdom Travel's 'Way of Life'.
TRAVELLER	*(His/her presence instantly giving her confidence)* I'm so glad to see you. I thought for a moment that I was on my own.
COURIER	Once you get started you'll never be on your own. I can promise you that. Now, if you will come with me.
	The TRAVELLER puts on her kit bag and starts pushing her trolley.
COURIER	Oh, is all that luggage yours?
TRAVELLER	I hope it's all right. I've been kitted-out by an old established firm.
COURIER	I can see that! The problem is that the entrance you have to go through is rather small.
	They come to a small opening which could have a sign reading 'No Camels'.
TRAVELLER	I'll never get through there. Can't I take my luggage round some other way?
COURIER	I'm afraid not. There is no other way. Look, leave your luggage behind, you'll have far less to worry about and you'll find all you need on the journey.
TRAVELLER	*(She is very torn now and clutches at the trolley)* How can I be sure? I've only got your word for it and anyway I've invested a great deal in this, I can't just dump it.
MAMMON 1	Of course you can't.
MAMMON 2	Where would you be without your luggage?
COURIER	Leave it and go through the entrance. You'll never regret it.
MAMMON 1	Hold on! *(Showing their true nature in the next two speeches)*
MAMMON 2	Yes, hold on. You MAKE them take your luggage. How could you go without it?
TRAVELLER	I, I don't know what to do. I want to go, but I don't want to leave my luggage *(Desperately to COURIER)* Well, surely you can help me?
COURIER	It's your choice. No one else can make it for you. You've got to choose one way or the other.

TRAVELLER	I want to go, but . . .

And there we leave the TRAVELLER, though the AGENTS come forward to have the last word.

MAMMON 1	What happens next?
MAMMON 2	Will she let go her luggage?
MAMMON 1	Or keep it and come with us after all?
BOTH	Don't miss the next thrilling instalment of − Travel Agency!

Talking Point

Do we really have to make the choice between the luggage provided by 'Mammon Tours' and travelling the 'Way of the Kingdom'? In what particular manner might this choice face us?

THE MAGIC SOUP

Production Note
Everything in this sketch turns on the villagers moving from 'I haven't got anything to spare' to WANTING to put something in the pot. It is ideal for a Family Service where extra children or adults can be involved in the bringing of ingredients for the soup. You will need a large cooking pot and all the various items that will go into it, not forgetting the six inch nail. No need to overdo the realism. Fire and water are not essential!

Biblical Background
Deuteronomy 15.7−11, Be open-handed.
Luke 6.38, Give and it shall be given and many other passages about sharing what God has provided.

This sketch is written for six characters but a number of others could be, and hopefully would be, incorporated to bring additional ingredients for the soup. The extra players would need a minimum of rehearsal.

NARRATOR	*(Entering and addressing the audience)* I want to take you back to an afternoon a few years ago. Are you sitting comfortably? Right. *(He snaps his fingers)* We're there. It didn't hurt did it? *(He looks at his watch)* The time's about 4.30. No, I'm not saying 16.30, we don't hold with these new-fangled ways in our village. There's lots of other things we don't hold with in our village . . . like strangers. And sure enough I see one coming. He'll not get much of a welcome, I can tell you.
STRANGER	*(Entering through the audience)* Afternoon, friend; is there somewhere I might get a meal here?
NARRATOR	Well, I wouldn't like to say. You can always try. Never any harm in trying. Why not ask those women over there.
STRANGER	Why not indeed. Thank you kindly. I'll see you again. *(He goes across to the WOMEN, a little apart from the*

NARRATOR	*who are not gossiping, but each doing her own separate thing. They could be seated, knitting or mending)*
NARRATOR	See him again? Maybe, maybe not. He'll do well if he gets a meal here. *(He stands aside and watches the action develop)*
STRANGER	Good evening ladies. I've been walking all day and I'm just wondering whether one of you good souls could provide me with a meal.
FIRST WOMAN	Oh, I don't think I could do that.
SECOND WOMAN	I don't have spare food.
THIRD WOMAN	You see, we're very poor people.
FOURTH WOMAN	I don't know where I'm going to get a meal for my own family tonight, let alone anybody else.
THIRD WOMAN	No, I don't either.
SECOND WOMAN	You'd really do better to look some place else.
STRANGER	Are you telling me that things are so bad that you really can't find a little food for a traveller. Surely, there's someone in the village . . .?
FIRST WOMAN	No, we're all in the same condition.

We see the STRANGER continuing the conversation as the NARRATOR speaks again.

NARRATOR	You see what I mean. It's always the same. He'll be on his way any minute now.

The NARRATOR, steps back again and the conversation continues.

STRANGER	Well, well, well. Since you're all so poor that you can't do anything for me, I'd better see if I can't do something for you.
SECOND WOMAN	You're joking. What could you do for us?
THIRD WOMAN	You haven't got anything; else you wouldn't be asking us for a meal.
FOURTH WOMAN	Go on, tell us. What could you do?
STRANGER	What would you say if I made a rich soup, enough for everyone in the village?
FIRST WOMAN	You could do that. Without any help?
STRANGER	No, I'll need help of course . . .
SECOND WOMAN	I knew there was a catch in it.

36

STRANGER	I'll tell you the help I'll need. I'll need the loan of a large cooking pot, big enough for us all; I'll need some firewood and of course I'll need some water.
THIRD WOMAN	How will you do it?
STRANGER	Lets leave that for the moment. The first question is, are you prepared to provide the cooking pot, the fire and the water?
FOURTH WOMAN	The children would soon gather some firewood.
SECOND WOMAN	There's plenty of water in the pump.
FIRST WOMAN	You can use a cooking pot that came to me from my mother. It's too big for our family, but I always keep it clean.
STRANGER	Then that's all we need.
FOURTH WOMAN	All you need?
THIRD WOMAN	How are you going to do it, you can't make soup using just water.
STRANGER	Of course I can't. No, I shall use this. *(He produces a large nail from his pocket)*
FOURTH WOMAN	*(Looking at it closely)* It's a nail. It's just an old six-inch nail.
STRANGER	It is indeed a nail, but it is not just any old nail. This is a magic nail.
WOMEN	*(Backing away)* Magic!
STRANGER	No need to be frightened. It is magic in one thing only. It makes beautiful soup.

> *During the NARRATOR's next speech the fire and the cooking pot are set in place and the WOMEN gather round to watch the STRANGER at work. At this point others might join them.*

NARRATOR	Well, an hour's gone by. It's five thirty now and he's got them real excited at the idea of free soup. What's that? You want to know whether we're really as poor as the women made out?. We haven't got all that much, but we get by. I suppose our biggest problem is that we keep ourselves so much to ourselves. Can't think when I last saw folks together like this. Mind you, I wouldn't like to say what would happen if he doesn't come up with the goods.
STRANGER	We're on the way. Time to put the nail in. Here goes. *(He*

	puts the nail into the pot) Now we've just got to wait.
FIRST WOMAN	And you don't add anything else at all?
STRANGER	When you're really poor you can't, can you? Of course, on some occasions I've been able to add a little salt and pepper, but . . .
FIRST WOMAN.	I can get some salt and pepper.
STRANGER	If you're really sure.
FIRST WOMAN	I'm not as poor as all that. *(She goes)*
STRANGER	*(To the others)* That's a bonus isn't it. It'll improve the flavour no end. *(He makes himself comfortable, then starts reminiscing)* I remember one evening on such a village green, there was someone who actually found a couple of turnips.
SECOND WOMAN	I could spare a turnip or two.
STRANGER	Could you now, really? Are you sure? *(SECOND WOMAN goes)*
THIRD WOMAN	Would a few carrots be any use? *(Going)*
FOURTH WOMAN	I've a couple of onions. *(Also goes)*

> *If there are people available to swell the cast other voices could come in offering other vegetables and some meat bones.*

STRANGER	We don't want to spoil the distinctive flavour of the nail of course, but, no, we could take your offers, that'll be fine; *(Calling after them)* but you'd better hurry along if we're to eat it tonight. *(One by one they return with various gifts for the pot)*
NARRATOR	Six o'clock. And what a transformation. I've never seen the village so alive; and look what's going into that pot. *(He names the various ingredients as they are added one by one to the soup)*
STRANGER	*(When all is in)* Well, that's good. Now all we need is something to stir it with.
FIRST WOMAN	I thought you'd realise that sooner or later. Here, I've brought this ladle, it'll do for serving too.
STRANGER	Thank you. *(He takes it and stirs gently)* Just a matter of time now.

> *As the NARRATOR speaks those around the pot are miming smelling the aroma and talking happily together.*

38

NARRATOR	So a couple of hours pass, seven o'clock, eight o'clock. People have begun to enjoy each other's company. It's never happened like this before and all the time the smell of the soup wafting over the green.
STRANGER	That's it I think. *(He tastes it)* Excellent! Have you each got a bowl with you? Good. *(He starts serving)*
NARRATOR	And there I think we'd better leave it folks, and return to the present time, after all, it's not much fun watching other people eat. *(He snaps his fingers and says to the cast)* Off you go. *(They exit. The NARRATOR addresses the audience again)* So, we're back. It was a good soup I can tell you, a real rich meal in itself. And it's a funny thing, but we were a different village afterwards. Somehow that night the old suspicion and isolation all went. We haven't seen the stranger again, though we often speak of him. *(He pauses for a moment then continues)* It was a marvellous soup he made for us and we've never got over the fact that he did it all with just one six inch nail.

Talking Point

This is not so much about giving as about sharing; about learning to be a true community. What application has it for you? Locally? Nationally? Internationally?

Other Titles from RADIUS and NCEC

THE HILL
Sylvia Read
0-7197-0761-7

A modern mystery play in which the characters find themselves caught up in the experience of Easter. 30 mins.

Code No. PLA0761 (A)

CROSSTALK
Bob Irving
0-7197-0795-1

A collection of ten short plays based upon the parables which were, in their own time, sharp contemporary stories in an established tradition. In order to convey the same sense of immediacy these sketches are presented in a highly modern quick-firing style. No need for props or costumes, maximum cast of five. Each play lasts about 5 minutes.

Code No. PLA0795 (A)

SURPRISE SKETCHES
Ronald Rich
0-7197-0796-X

Five one-act plays with surprising endings. Ideal as a prompter for discussion or for use in worship, these plays examine some familiar human failings in a new stimulating style. Each play runs for about 10 minutes.

Code No. PLA0796 (A)

THE FLAME
Edmund Banyard
0-7197-0709-9

A novel approach to the idea of Pentecost, this play is a one act fantasy in the style of the Theatre of the Absurd. Four ordinary people are offered the 'Light of the World' by a messenger from the border between Time and Eternity. 25 mins.

Code No. FLA0709 (A)

> Performance times given are
> very approximate.

A FISTFUL OF FIVERS
Edmund Banyard
0-7197-0667-X

Twelve five-minute plays, each with a Christian message. Using the minimum of actors, scenery and props, these lively sketches will appeal to everyone who is young in the widest sense.

Code No. PLA0667 (A)

A FUNNY THING HAPPENED ON THE WAY TO JERICHO
Tom Long
0-7197-0722-6

The dress rehearsal for a presentation of the Good Samaritan turns out to be more than the leading player intended, as she is challenged by each of the roles she takes on in her search for the one she feels happy with. 30 mins.

Code No. FUN0722 (A) R

THE PRODIGAL DAUGHTER
William Fry
0-7197-0668-8

Using a neat twist, William Fry has turned one of the best-known parables into the tale of a present-day girl, updating the setting to portray some of the concerns of modern society. While it shows the seamier side of contemporary life, the message of this play is ultimately one of redemption and love. 30 mins.

Code No. PLA0668 (A)

NATIVITY LETTERS
Nick Warburton
0-7197-0724-2

Highlights the strains put on mother and daughter in the interdependence of a single parent family, which make them tend to disassociate themselves from other people. Help eventually presents itself through a committed teacher in the daughter's drama group. 40 mins.

Code No. NAT0724 (A)

WHO'LL BE BROTHER DONKEY?
Arthur Scholey
0-7197-0723-4

Three traditional Christmas tales are combined to produce this play where the animals use their Christmas Eve gift of speech to enact the crib scene in the hillside chapel. During the journey from their stable they outwit the wily Fox and Vixen in their malevolent schemes. The conclusion shows how the preparation of the crib scene is achieved against all odds through forgiveness of their fellow creatures and faith. 60 mins.

Code No. WHO0723 (A)